SONG
OF AN
ALIEN

Over 130 Poems of Love,
Romance, Passion, Politics,
and Life in its Complexity

CHARLES MWEWA

iUniverse, Inc.
New York   Bloomington

SONG OF AN ALIEN

Over 130 Poems of Love, Romance, Passion, Politics, and Life in its Complexity

iUniverse books may be ordered through booksellers or by contacting:

iUniverse
1663 Liberty Drive
Bloomington, IN 47403
www.iuniverse.com
1-800-Authors (1-800-288-4677)

ISBN: 978-1-4401-1678-0 (pbk)
ISBN: 978-1-4401-1679-7 (ebk)

Printed in the United States of America
iUniverse rev. date: 1/9/09

For

Charles Calder

CONTENTS

ABOUT CHARSIAN POETRY

Words have beautiful sounds. Poetry adds sense to these beautiful sounds. Poetry is therefore sound and sense in verse. Poetry touches the heart first before it hits the paper! It is the song of the heart actualized through codified symbols.

Song of an Alien is a collection of some of the poems I have written in the period of twelve years. It covers a variety of themes ranging from romance to pain, from ecstasy to soul matters, and from political to social issues, in all their complexities. The style employed in my work is what I call the Charsian Poetry, which I have acquired over a passage of close to ten years. It is a mixture of rhyme and blank in free verse. Charsian Poetry is the exposition of reality. Surrealism has its own place, but a good poem is an input to what transpires in the day to day lives of human beings. It is a contribution to reality. The world is never the same once a good poem has been added.

I love poetry. At the University of Zambia (UNZA)a group of us came together and formed a poetry club. Charles Calder, a Scottish professor of literature and language and a friend (to who this book is dedicated), was a huge influence on my development and appreciation of poetry. In 2000 Charles and I directed Elizabethan drama for the British Council and influenced a young generation of poets. I hope that everyone reading these poems will enjoy them the way I enjoyed writing them.

The book is divided into five sections referred to as "Books." Each Book has a number of poems related thematically. Book One is quintessentially romance. Book Two is a spontaneous reaction to lost love, memory and hope. Book Three contains poems dealing with our duty to state, to human rights and to one another. Book Four is a long narrative poem addressed to the Aushi tribe of Zambia. It is a celebration of libido and the beauty of womanhood. Book Five contains forty songs of an alien, a symbolic character who reflects on moral, political and cultural matters.

An alien, a foreigner, from elsewhere
alienated from his own people,
his kind, his color, his race;
alienated in mind and in deed,
isolated from the support and
the sympathy of those he is familiar with.

BOOK ONE

LOVE SUPREMACY

They love too much that die for love

- English Proverb

1| My Love, I

My love warms me when I am cold,
She means to me more than pure gold
She knows the secrets of my soul
And with her I can't long for more

She will delight and fullfil me
My love is but the good I see
He is the soul within my soul;
In his arms I gladly give all

Be closer than breath, all my days
Be a friend I trust, in all ways
Put your arms around me, all night
And guard my nude heart, from all sight

Come to me, I die without you
Each day I wait for your true feel
Take out from my eyes all my tears
And rid my heart of pain and fears

2| My Love, II

My love hides me from the sun's heat
In her kind voice mind and soul beat
She thrills like the sun in the sky
And stills like moonlight lullaby

I feel bounds of raging tenses
And miss my love with five senses.
My soul does languish with plight,
Yet our hearts flourish with delight

In the depth of quiet reflections,
Rhythms of my roused recollections
Rhyme to the sound of his name
For to love and rescue me he came

In your soul my whole being belongs
My drained heart for you alone longs
Come to me, my love, come to me!
All you want, to you I will be

3| **Fondest Memories, I**

It was cool, calm, cold and clean

Down Keele to buy ice-cream

Hand in hand, we walked

With rare sacredness, we talked.

Love is a living thing, they say

Which no words can say,

No mind can understand,

And no soul can comprehend.

I love you, and I cannot explain it

Because loving you is pleasurable.

I love you, and I don't know why,

For loving you is easy, that's why.

You are everything that I want

More than the oil wells of Mid East;

More than the diamonds of Africa

More than the gold of America!

4| Fondest Memories, II

Since we parted, it has been hard.

And partings cost us everything.

I admit, I am not strong,

And you can not be too wrong

Lonely like an island

Absence breaks our hearts

Could I and you now just agree?

Our love is hurt by some degree?

I will follow you through the rains

Because my heart belongs to you,

Come; let us meet like two ways

And promise never to part ways!

5| Fondest Memories, III

My bride, my black lover:

To you this music I bring

From rhythms in my soul

I beat for you in cords of twos
And record for you a melody

Of a revolutionary orchestra

My bride, my youthful hart:

Dearly loved and treasured,

Your temperament is phlegmatic;

Cool, quiet and beautiful!

You are fair, my love, you are fair.

You have no flaw in you.

Your eyes are doves

And your lips drop honey.

For you, my heart beat in harmony.

Oh, catch for me my dear doe;

Let me rejoice all night long

And feel the warmth,
The power of two sweet loves.

6| Fondest Memories, IV

You are the wife of my
dreams

A friend closer than a
brother

Together we stick like a
letter

And follow each other like
shadows.

Like a hare trotting on the
Drakensburg, you came
along

Lovely to behold, soothing
to touch

And your eyes met mine,
and our hearts agreed, that
we belonged together.

Days go like flakes in the
sky

And night comes rushing in

In your heart are red roses

Whence I spread a bed of
our deep romance

My wife glitters like
the sun;

In her boson reason
and emotions
harmonize

And bring meaning to a life

on its last legs.

7| Fondest Memories, V

Your eyes are a
thoroughfare

Straight like a pine
tree

Your face
thoroughly shines
as one who has been
to the fellowship of
angels

I wonder why all
such beauties aren't
at gun-point robbed!

Why were you
made thus bonbon?

Why do I crave for
you with psychotic
lunacy?

Why does sleep
leave me at the
thought of you?

Why do I gaze at
you like a newly
born baby?

Your lips drip of
vanilla

Your borders in
chocolate drawn –

Your tongue of
cinnamon brand,

Your heart, a
sanctuary of gods!

8| Fondest Memories, VI

Your shape
is a dream of
knighted lords

Shaped through
fragile contours

You are curved
as a god in
Aphrodisiac
casing

With such a
small waist on
ivory-paired
legs

I wonder why
such tiny feet
support such
frail figures!

Your hand
tender, soft as
sponge

As splendid as
taintless gold

The back of
your yard

Couth and
carefully
cultivated

Arranged as
twins of the
same design

9| Fondest Memories, VII

Thy gyrations doth move mine entrails

Thy neck long, soft and vivid…

Thy embrace in mine arms grips

How comfy and delightful!

Fools doth attest to thy beauty

The strong doth faint in thy presence

The wise in thy breath words deny

Bragging men and loafers thou loath

Thy head with wit brims

Thy mind with brilliance rims

Thy faculties with reason drone

Thy hairs full, long and grown

Thy make-up, costly and lavish

Thy men's spirits thou crush

Thy equals labors thou render null

And thine rivals cry foul

10| Veronice

This heart has made a clever choice,
With these lips we utter a voice
Of our lovely Veronice,
A girl so sweet and very nice

She heals like a veronica
And cures like a santonica;
She is a clear memoranda
Of issues on observanda

Hard to face as a facular
She glitters as a nebula.
Her flesh is all fresh synovia
In red roses of Monrovia

We composed her a fantasia
Imported from Eastern Asia
To be rubbed with spices of India
In charmed scents of Parafindia

11| Chara

I knew it that very first time
When I looked at your smiling face
And reasoned you were in your prime,
Even so I thought I could chase.

Chara, I love you with my whole heart

And time came for being closer friends
I knew it was not a mistake
For it wasn't like we could be fiends
When there was so much at stake.

Chara, my love for you is pure art

12| My Face

I recall the first time I saw you.
Since then so many things have happened
And that early excitement has gone.

There comes in one's life a time and season,
When the first bunch of roses fades
And only dry memories remain.

On these scattered memories, my love
I have dutifully spread a bed
With a pillow top of dead rose leaves.

Many times beauty is deceptive
And charm, a passing wave of the wind
And only inner chaste makes life sure

For always my face in yours I see
This I call faultless Epiphany
When in your beauty, mine I see, too.

13| Till I Have You

Not till I have you, will I rest,
Not till you become my sole quest,
Not till the drums beat at their best
Not till I rise to be the first
And riffraff turn into champions,
Will I be your soul companion

I'll not detour by matters of shame
Nor divert by flashes of fame
The sting of the rose may prickle
The rays of the sun may sparkle
You and I shall reach the summit
And there we shall glow very bright.

You dream of the team of the best
And not till you're mine, shall I rest

14| Jenevive

She is only called Jenevive.

Her bosom is the King's armor.
She mixes the tastiest of soups,
Prepares the cleanest of chambers
And wears the widest of all smiles.

She possesses the grace of does
And struts with the pride of male lions.

Her womb bears the healthiest babies
And her man married the noblest.

She is only called Jenevive.

15| Stronger Than Death

She dies softly and slowly,
The lady in a song
Of pure love:

Her eyes small and dizzy
Her touch gentle and lazy
She gazes by the eye sides
With hidden black pupils.

When she is fully cuddled
She dies in the ramblings
Of the seventh heaven
And whispers in overtones of love.

When she feels the flow
Of living streams,
She grumbles meaningless promises,
And demands she be tightly held.

Then sense and reason
Doubly crash with a bung,
Bone and marrow mar the bounds
And hands and words
Become one!

There is no feeling greater
No orgasmic sensation better
No life sweeter
And a death so fair and swifter!

16| Till the Bells

Honey,
They are saying we are not strong
And they are all wrong.

Honey,
Because they don't know the truth
About the values we hold dear
That we have been through the fire
And have come out pure.

Honey,
But they may be right
Because it may happen after a fight
That their vows couples don't hold tight
And of their duty they may lose sight.

Honey,
Our love is like a rock,
In the middle of Lake Michigan;
Waters rise and on shores knock
Yet it never goes back where it began.

Honey,
Let them be talking
And let's keep walking!

17| Look at Her

She climbs down the stairways of Toronto
My woman who walks on ivory legs.

A sheer glance perturbs even the stronger
And the most alert of minds.

Her moves are a dance and her steps are tempos
Beaten by invisible skill.

The capture of her bosom yields peace and fire
And her eyes sparkle with shining glory.

She gold-chains her neck and ring crafts her ankles
And garbs herself in red garments.

Look at the woman, I say
Look at her and afterwards pray.

18| Gold

I was not dreaming about gold
Nor hallucinating of gold
I swerved on my bed and saw gold
Before me were presents of gold,
My eyes ogled at pure gold
And she was admirable gold.

My words came out simple and clear
And I could hear them too clearly;
They sprung with brilliant clarity:

She is in her very own class
The best out of seven classes
And first in her beauty classroom.

And the all parade shouted: "gold"
Then the echo grew loud and bold
Passing in gaps of heat and cold
Bracing the memories of old,
Bringing out great pleasures untold
Priceless treasures never to be sold.

19| My Darling

My darling is first with daughters
A gem washed with holy waters
She reads classics of ancient books
And only dates men with good looks

My darling is an example
Of a star reared in the tempo
Of superb divine conception
Where angels man her reception

Daughters of the brave and the mighty
Gathered to placate Aphrodite
With their complicated hair-dos
And she beat them clearly in twos

Daughters of nations, far and near
Come and get her charm, true and dear
And she will teach and show them all
In Athena's decked palace mall

20| Marry at 30

Most of them marry at 25
That's when things move, *mwana*.
Dreams now are all the same
And strength is overwhelming.

I tell you marry at 30
That's when reason fails,
Dreams have all ceased
And feelings do not overwhelm.

There is a struggle now, *mwana*.
With warm burning passions
And relief plays very far
Serve to just marry, *mwana.*

Do not add another year, *mwana*.
Two, three or more years
You will become insane
And lose the flavor of life.
.
At 30 marry your woman, *mwana.*

21| Love You So Much

Hello, darling, they are saying:
"He loves her like his sister"
But they also brag that you love me.
They say that we talk alike.
They shudder that we have passion.
They say that it flows so natural.
They compare us to the two elbows
And always demand for an answer.

They do not know the secret, darling.
Though eyes they have, they don't see.
They know not that love given
Is the love that one receives.
When I hold you closest to me,
Then natural grace points at you
And I praise your natural splendor.

22| Yours is Chubby

I will sing you this song
With no wit of poetry.
Because of your deep rift
And your chubbiness.

You have planted an orchard
In the form of a triangle
And in the middle of which
Is a living fountain
With a warmth of wet heat.

At the lips
You plant sweetness
And in your mouth
Are watermelons
You have apples in your eyes
And garlands of ivory
In your legs.

But the middle and fundament
That guard of heightened sensors
That takes the brain of a child
And turns it into manhood
Is the prize of the well-bred.

23| Love Songs

My bride and my cherished love
From the rhythms of my heart
I create concertos in tunes
I beat dual codes
And for you
I record
Songs

My cute bride is my dear hart
She is kind and gorgeous
She is fair and dear
She takes my heart
And brings joy
With love
Songs

My mom once told me to hear
The words of my love's beat
And not to dare miss
The true meaning
Of love themes
Veiled in
Songs

My dad was not wrong at all
When he told me to learn
To hear and perceive
What is unsaid
By my dear
In love
Songs

24| Beside Me

I would have thought "Mary"
When besides me sat a figure
The aura on her head
And the precious visage
Were out of this world
Her labia dripped honey,
Pure from the honeycomb.

The space between her chest
Was narrow, lubricated scented fluid
And proudly comforted men.

The styles embedded hairs
Would have given expert saloons
Great difficulties in phathomation
In my subconscious I fainted
Till the one besides me left
Then I wondered how that
Beauty is no respecter of reason.

25| No Capacity

If looks could kill
My eyes would be long dead.
We see in part
But then the entire thing
And he who cannot perform
Is not fortunate.

The crow cries "No capacity"
When a guy fails to bring his lady to ice

The hare with curiosity asked:
"Foolish vultures, why kill
And fail to eat?"

The saint remarked:
"I married, not buried!"

So are the sounds of life
Soaring with vibes of life
Socking all the pains of life
Soaking all the juices in life.

26| Clarice

Clarice your eyes are little doves
The brand even mighty Zeus loves;
They have been fashioned from above
And given to us all in love.

Clarice your cute eyes are gracious
Certainly full-size and precious
While clearly round and capacious
Yet brownish and very spacious.

Clarice your eyes do shine brightly
With pupils well placed just rightly
To allow heat only slightly
And endow with sight delightly.

Clarice is decked in color red
Sight very well tidy and bred
That the cowardly dash in dread
Yet her acumen is well spread.

27| Miracles of Love

Babies used to be miracles of love
When people in their simplicity
Did not use science and drugs
To stop the fusion of ripe cells.

Death used to be a stranger
When people in their simplicity
Did not use science and drugs
To stop the spread of infections.

A boy in the presence of love
Shall force the growing of beards.
Babies and more babies
And cessation of monthly cycle
Are all miracles of love.

Birth and marriage and death
Are all miracles of this life
Even when men conquer them
They are still miracles of love.

28| Love to Remember

I remember…
And skies testify.
My heart leaped.
I remember…
Your young long face
Of which poets are fond of-
Kin sister to morning star.
I know no beauty as yours.

I remember…
The feeling and the taste…
The view and pictures.

I remember …
A mind made up,
A fearless resolve
And the risky trips.

I remember…
Love greater than life
And your tender graces.

I remember…your love.

29| Love Can Build a Bridge

Love can build a bridge
Between your heart and mine

Love can erect a passage
In the conflict of many interests.

Love can construct a canal
In the midst of witlessness.

Love can make the sky blue
In the place of gloom and dullness.

Love can dig a long tunnel
And reach to wonderful lands.

Love can build a bridge
Between your heart and mine.

30| Tashany's Song

Thank you, for my kids
Thank you, for the joy that they bring
Thank you, for dark nights
That they turn into mourning
And grey days they turn to white.

Thank you, for the privilege
Thank you, for life they lavish with purpose,
Hope they bring to shattered dreams,
And furious storms they calm with peace.

Thank you, for the miracle
Thank you, for the tender shoots
Thank you, for the innocent pulsing hearts
Sleeping silently in see-saw cribs
Surrounded by angels and perking wings.

Thank you, for second chances
For in them, loafing drives emerge
And frustrated opportunities surface again.
In them, mooching ideas emasculated
Rise to the test of hope
To bring forth attitudes kind and dear.

Thank you, for this love
That no mind can grasp
And no intellect can clasp.

31| A Mother's Love

Mother, because you have a mother's love

Other loves do not match a mother's love.

Together, let's cherish a mother's love.

Hither-to earth stands on a mother's love.

Either we choose war or a mother's love.

Rather than gold, trade with a mother's love!

32| Amanda

There is a place truer than nature
An abode fairer than paradise
In the inner chamber therein
All dearest memories
Of things said and unsaid
Do find boundless expressions.

There is a person known to us
More than we know our palm
Whose voice rings music to us,
And whose countenance strikes
A breath-taking enigma.

There is a love, deeper than bliss
A feeling soother than a kiss
A person more desirable than peace
And a name we'll never miss.

Like her sweet name, Amanda,
Oh, is it just a dream, I wonder!

BOOK TWO

HEARTCRY

Sorrow is better than laughter; for by the sadness of the countenance the heart is made better

-Ecclesiastes 7:3

33| Painful Thought

There is a beauty so much dear
A person who so moves thine life
That thou art made to drop a tear;
To breed grief wherein rage is rife

She puts elements in thine soul
The eternal chip that so stings
That thine physical being, and more
From this point forward moves and springs

Beauty is who she plainly is
Bright as the fullest morning star
For the real package is all his
To cause avowed foes hard to spar

She beams with eyes of love and peace,
High weights of concern and vain fights
So weave jointly into one piece,
That thine hurtly ego within frights

This smile that thou have, O dearest
Takes ruthless tolls on myriad minds
And breathes shivers without rest;
That thy nimble limb wobbly winds!

A painful thought, O flawless Ruth
In exile a prince thou rejected
Till late thou stumbled on the truth;
Still, thou art missed; how dejected!

34| Ashen Pebbles

The hilarity of them who thump through the thumb
Of ashen pebbles;
In which they thrum through the stricken crumb
Of sunken fables;
The thrill of them whose thrust falls on numb
Aces of shrunken tables;
Who hung the tongue of a slyly throated lamb
With molten cables

These hard earned medals will only be metals
Damned to the ghettoes;
These blooms subjected to a loom of broken petals
Gammed without vetoes;
These garlands from the land of our twisted sepals,
Our Jammed mementoes;
And the stories of our glories deified in the temples
Of hammed potentials

A throne thrown in jumbled destinations
By a confederation of nations,
These high hopes of childhood hijacked by fate,
Becoming the coveted bait of hate;
And the gentle voice of discrimination
Breeds consternation
In blanket canopied hearts of immigrants,
Enslaved by the lavish junkets of grants

35| Words of the Departed

Words of the departed loved ones
Will not be forgotten.
Even though they have long left us,
Their words still ring new life.

Like a parrot, we rewind them
And repeat them oftenly.
For they bring sweet memories
Of times and joys we shared.

That sad and gloomy day of loss
When death's messenger knocks,
With these remembrances of love,
We drown them and move on.

36| Do not Cry

I heard you when you cried
And your face said it all:
"Mommy I miss you," you said
And your voice fainted.

And these words, unedited
Followed, unscripted:

"I feel rejected in this world
Where you have left me.
Mommy, you left me alone.
You were there for me always.
There is no-one by my side.
I miss your kindness
Rest in peace, dear mom."

I was there when you cried
And offered my hank
Then you dried.

37| Dirge of My People

The dirge my people cry,
Oh, these songs they sing
When loved ones are gone
Are full of sorrows
When they are sung.

When they lament silently,
"Oh you people without mercy,
You have grabbed Chandwe
For no reason at all."

These bring grief and regret
Which touch the soul.

My people dance as they mourn
And sing rhythms of grief.
Their limbs barely move
When sorrow, melody and pain
Are mixed in the pot of loss.

The dirges my people cry;
To placate their dead they try!

38| Friends Gone

Our few days are told as a tale
A remorse fact I now must tell.
Once you hear that pitiless bell;
It has destiny turning pale.

I do recall a few loved friends
Who lamely met their story ends
After that human's nasty fiend,
Their life he denied to extend.

Surely every good turns to waste
When winds bluster by way of west;
Again people have failed their test
For none comes to detail past taste.

While our deceased leave a picture,
And a voice of their departure,
Sorrow is not a good teacher,
Nor sorry a better preacher.

39| Goodbye to Daddy

Mama never seemed to miss
The finer things of life
If she did
She never did say so to daddy.

She never wanted to be more than
A mother and a wife
If she did
She never did say so to daddy.

The only thing that seemed to be
Important in her life
Was to make our house a home
To make us happy.

Mama never wanted any
More than what she had
If she did
She never did say so to daddy.

And she never missed the flowers
And the cards he never sent her
If she did
She never did say so to daddy.

The thing he took for granted
Was the thing that she accepted
And she didn't need those things
To make her happy.

And she didn't seem to notice
That he didn't kiss or hold her
If she did
She never did say so to daddy.

One morning we awoke
Just to find a note
Mama carefully wrote
And left for daddy.

And receiving and reading
Our ears could not believe it
The words she had written there for daddy.

She said the kids are now old
They don't need me very much
Now I can go and search for the love
I need so badly.

Goodbye to daddy.

40| Goodbye to Sara

Joshua used to ignore
The sleeps of her tongue
And Sara never minded
How she used her language.

She told Joshua a story
Of her past date with Peter
And Sara never minded
How she used her language.

One day she told him
That Peter was better a guy
And Sara never minded
How she used her language.

She said Peter was rich
And gave her all she wanted
And Sara never minded
How she used her language.

And Sara told Joshua
To dress like old boyfriends did
And Sara never minded
How she used her language.

One day Joshua met Jane;
Jane was down to earth
And Joshua was happy
Jane understood who Joshua was.

Joshua came back to Sara
To say that it was over
Because Sara never minded
How she used her language.

Goodbye to Sara.

41| The Grip

Dark Shadow
It comes to all like a shadow
And beckons us to enter the door
To take us through eternal meadow
To places prepared for all.

Endless Journey
Though no one may clearly say
How far on this journey to stay
By the flurries of a clear day
We know they don't return our way.

Abode
The spirits of those who depart
For so nature that knows in part
Does tell us they are set apart
For places known by the expert.

Trespass
Though your power in trespass be
One has triumphed over thee
To make safe passage for you and me
When our eyes are closed we see.

Hope
They go each to their very end
In doubt we may know or pretend
But know we in peace they spend
Their rest,
And in hope their faults mend.

42| Elegy to Kenya

O Kenya, hide thy bloody face
And look not on thy bloody mess
Because thy recrimination
Has trodden many a nation.

Thou art now insensitive
To the plight of thy own children
And for women, thou'nt perceptive
For in their ruin thy terrors reign.

By thine western end Eldoret
Thirty-three innocents perish
Butcher'ed at a brutal rate
While skulls prayed in a deaf parish.

Many voices are heard far away
Yet here they fall on aching trust
And no reason will dare to sway
The shame of man's deadly past.

Drums in Africa are beating,
And the children are not dancing.
Women endure in child labor,
To enter worlds they will abhor.

In a butcher's slaughtering sword,
Elections are but a by-word;
And democracy's sunny face
Is mired in anarchy's dire race.

And for the fair arm of the law,
Guns rule and danger guard the poll
While old regimes cling to power,
To destroy liberty's tower.

43| Destiny Killers

Pain runs through his veins
Like a sharp end of a dagger.
Thoughts came out dense
And words were few.

He remembers the dream
He had for his next of kin.
He took his time and money
And worked only for her.

He bought her all school needs
And saved for her college.
He moved her to a better place,
Away from destiny killers.

She broke the law of decency
When she disregarded his efforts;
She met her destiny killer
And cut her destiny short.

44| Women

Women:
They were meant to be loved
Their bodies look like
They were meant to be loved
Their voices sound like
They were meant to be loved
Their eyes shine like
They were meant to be loved
Their mouths speak like
They were meant to be loved
Their stories tell like
They were meant to be loved
They are weaker than men
For they were meant to be loved
They are made from inside out
Because they were meant to be loved
They have a nature
Soft and hard
That's why they have to be loved
They possess the sweetness
Of honey
But they sting like bees
To show that they were meant to be loved
They walk with a lion's pride
Gyrate with peacock's vanity
Think with a serpent's sharpness
Relate with chameleon skills
Attract like a magnet
And kill with a scorpion's venom.

It is a verity,
Women were meant to be loved!

45| Life in Circles

Yesterday remains white;
Today it's green
And tomorrow is black.

Life in circles.

In memory lanes we drive
Today your son
And tomorrow your guardian.

Life's imperfidious visage.

We eat, drink and clothe,
We loaf, work and shelter,
That is all there is to life.

Life in circles.

And the unexpected happens:
Servants become bosses
Girls become boys
Beggars become lenders
And hours become minutes.

But when men marry men
Days turn to nights
And it snows all day non-stop;

The circles just continue.

46| Secure

In the middle of the bush
When you leave me behind
I feel very insecure.
When you come back
And talk to me like a friend,
I feel very secure.

When alone at the middle of bushes
Just a thought of you
Makes me secure again.
Whatever you say,
When we are in the thicket
I just believe
And in the shadow of your presence
All my fears just disappear.
I know I am under your care
I really feel very secure.

47| Mad

We all know madmen pick
They may pick up a treasure.
And sane men study
They may study how to die.
At night madmen sleep outside
And worry about nothing.

The sane also sleep at night
In the prison of their own fences.
Madmen pick in garbage bins
And sane men throw therein.

While the sane suffer from ulcers
Madmen never
Take sleeping pills!

Both do die and are forgotten.

48| Unfaithfulness

Once you hear of this word
"Unfaithfulness"
You know there are other things.
Once you become
"Unfaithful"
You know you have been others.
Once you are
"Unfaithful"
You know you've lost yourself.

It is dent to the best plan,
A cancer to healthy cells,
And a crack in one's soul.

49| **Cry We Cry**

There are many days when we fly
And surely some days we do cry.
There are things we hate and deny
Which our minds daily occupy.

The worst part of us when it comes
All joy and peace it never calms.
We hate it with perfect hatred
Leaving us very frustrated.

Why then is that our own nature
Is much difficult to nurture?
We have dual personalities
Competing for our priorities.

When we think that we have things right
Then our own dreams turn into night
And for our visions and desire
Only shame and pain we acquire.

Yet life must be better I know
For I know good things will be more,
And some day I shall reach glory
To tell my earned and true story.

50| Journey

The journey,
Will begin at Lusaka
Via Harare to
London to Toronto.

Tokyo
Guatemala City
Calgary
Joburg
And the world is conquered.

You can start yours
When you set up goals
Of the destiny you chose
To become your own boss!

51| Never to Forget

Mother,
How can I
How can I forget you?
Why should I
Why should I fail to remember
Mine months in your tummy?
Hopeless
Helpless.
Many times
You met with death in the noon.
You shielded me militantly
And delivered me alive.

Mother,
I forget you today,
I warrant failure
To remember
My own
Birthday.

52| Only Child

I have always known you

My only child.
Even that first day, in my womb
When you wiggled
And that first day on earth
When you giggled.
You will never know
How much joy I felt
The first time
You chuckled.
I always longed to see your face,
Shy, little and delicate;
I held you in my arms
Gave you the first kiss
And you waggled.

I will always love you
My only child.
I was first in your life.
My lips you kissed
And my breasts you sucked
And every time you left me
I jiggled.

You will always be
My only child.

53| Presidential Challenge

Gather you mighty and loyal
To the inaugural of the royal
For in their shadow we live and toil
While our own fate we foil.

The giant claws of mighty dragon
And we their subjects seethe in argon
Of our forgotten intellect
And dance to tunes for us they elect.

They murder more those by order
Than those at periphery of border
Who must plead self-defense
For crimes they only call offence.

A president I will, rather than king
For a precedent is only one thing
To follow the rule they create for him
To borrow peace and kill joy it seem.

There is one boy in all presidents
Who seek the camp of dissidents
To dissent the will of general deal
And rule according to general will.

54| Among Warriors

Days come and go
Each with subtle claws
On them are visages
And dark images.
I see with my mind
The danger they portend
But I hold on to my belief
And there is relief
That the humble sky
Towards where I fly
Shall some day be blue
And that is just as true.
The light shall appear
And like a sharp spear
Shall cut across barriers
To be named among warriors.

55| Dreams at Lusaka

The statement of one's life:
All in their early childhood
When they are growing up
Have moments of dreaming.

Dreams are not realities at all
And many dreams are sham.
But they plant divine seeds
On which fantasy thrives.

Fantasy itself is very lofty
Always creating impressions
And cosmetics borrow dearly
From illusions of our heads.

Statement are not the same:
They grow like dull flowers
Budding in wrong seasons
Breeding broken petals.

At Lusaka, home of rising stars
Where they emerge from obscurity
To dress in casual and coats
And dance to alien statements.

I want to be a star
The problem is just mine alone
And I share it with no one
Daring to walk the great path.

56| Our Name

A laborer's annual complaint:
I help others make great money
I escort money into other accounts
I defend the estates in others' names
And forget I have my own assets.

A laborer's complaint of a decade:
Now I have sons and daughters
I have bought them a house and cars
They go to good schools and churches
And I worry if they will succeed.

A laborer does not complain now:
I have a name I cannot recognize
I have existed for all wrong reasons
I have achieved trophies that haunt
But now I live for one name, "Ours."

57| Lost Feelings

What shall I compare life to?
Life is like curio making.
From raw trunks of trees
There come perfect images.
And like a painter does
Thinking in terms of colors
And artists in terms of lines.

So these feelings we once had
Now long gone and vanished
Can be remade and painted.
New stanzas can be arranged
New themes enacted
And the feeling of love
Does not die though it may fade.

What shall I allude life to?
It is like matter
Which is never lost
But can only be converted.
Like dry roses, so are old loves
Down we lay our heads
And there we love and dream again.

58| Lights at Christmas

The light burns brightly to the end.
All things look good and very calm.
And wild flowers invade the land
In the presence of mistletoe.

It is Christmas Day in Sameland
Children will open their presents
And sit rounding the twinkling tree
In red oversized pajamas.

This season is very special
And the songs are very unique
People everywhere share in joy
To bring true peace in a vexed world.

These parcels of assorted gifts
Long gathered carefully in thrift
And in malls the jingle bells ring
While kids hum from carols singing.

The poor and needy will reckon
With lack and shortage that beckon
But with help from joyful Santa
They will receive gifts and fanta.

59| Music in the Sky

I am amazed how that
Above the clouds
That are above a gigantic ocean
Beats resounding melodies
In symphony of superb tunes
And sweet voice of Celine Deon,
And the electric vocals of Richie,
And the vibrancy of Cocker
Together with the beaming
Eloquence of Dolly-
How that these music go
On playing in the landless paths
In those heavens far above.
The sound so beautiful
In those snowy azures,
Bringing earthly pleasure.
These ecstasies are heavily pried for
When the listening becomes intense
And these beats flap the hips of the engine.
There is music in heaven
Bright and beautiful
Drawing a soothing feeling of laughter.
In these skies the busy-ness of life
And the pressure of brewing
Are all swallowed up
Compacted and recycled
And hearts beat in chorus.
Nearing the soils
Melodies begin to faint,
These sweet waves,
Softer than the soul -
And still, there is music in the sky.

60| Bodies

They meet to dance in disco clubs
To rhythms of din and sounds unheard
Surrounded by fumes thick and dense
In squeezed scents of melting hot sweat.

Magnolia of silhouetted discs
Play upon dense magnets of volts.
Bodies jive half-naked to singles
While in pure pleasure they shindig.

Lights shine inside moving shadows
Boys flash out identity cards;
Men show off tattoo-tattered backs
And women carpet-comb in wines.

To life and death they toss dense fluids
To delight they tease lethal forms
But they cannot tell who whips them
Nor are they blinded by dim lights.

Throngs of mercurial bodies bump
Skeletons in skirts and pants move
While disc jockeys keep energy
To pick after-party bodily remains.

BOOK THREE

PATRONAGE ULTIMATUM

Who saves his country violates no law
(Napoleon I)

61| Apolitical Theory

Classics
Thou built reason's mind, O Plato,
Shaped brain's wit, thou Aristotle,
And deified politics divine
Whence St. Augustine's city doth shine!

Hobbes
Thou men, equal in body and mind
Court thee that kingly Leviathan
To appease thine life, short and poor
By these contracts, flawed and unsure

Locke
Thou nature in thy undressed state
Do in liberty instruct all;
Our labors with property rewards;
These laws our happiness awards

Machiavelli
Thou double-minds of earthly reign
Partly foxes, partly lions,
Thrust thy trust in beastly powers
To slay virtue on saintly towers

Rousseau
Thou art depraved, O thinking man
And thy good to thy nature tied;
Born free, yet everywhere in chains,
And in forced freedom thine trust earns

62| Hillsboro

Thou city of Hillsboro
By the embers of Wichita
Though thou art only a borough
In thine quiet street once veered a star

Thou art smaller by thy numbers
Yet thou grow the famous and rich
And rarely add to thy members
Desiring thy symbols to reach

Thy people proud and sufficient
Coldly hold to thy horn of race
Whence they gasp like a patient
Cancerously marred in the face

In thine churches emerge a song
Of penance for equality
Whence thy masses in oneness sing
To save thine renowned quality

63| Mibenge

Mibenge, I do remember,
It was here, the root of my roots;
Across the trans-border journey
Crossing the Luapula River.

I do remember my childhood
And our fishing in Mulonga
With all the thickets and bushes
And our ancestors in ashes.

We have come to Mibenge,
The place of childhood scenery
In our fondest memories byes
Where my own beloved father lies.

These earths calmly rest Ngalula
Next to my father's chummy breasts;
In here, I remember innocence.
For tears, unlike memories, dry

Mibenge, where men ever fade
And depart before they can grey.
Mibenge, I remember nuts
A treat only called *intwilo*.

64| Bye-Bye Bishop

The terrain still remain light brown
But we have put on a bright gown.
Several questions of whether
It is only in good weather
That to noble men with big farms
We soon empty all in our arms?

The factual hour will always come
For troubled and torn hearts to calm
And never again to bishops
Will we exist to place our hopes.

We were not meant to live like them
We too have to fulfill our term.
Yet your prayer, O man of God
I will seek in lands far and cold.

65| Mother Zambia

Mother…
Of mound display
An unexplored Eden in Africa;
Full of Nature's best
And an endless of tradition…
(To Zambezi -
To pay an invocative visit:
The people on superstitious gravity)
To you Mother…
Higher vows I pay.
Your soils are veins of life,
The peace
The Joy
The resting
Your people, my people,
Occupied
In structures of thatch
And decorated mad walls!
Your idyllic terrains;
Much more unexploited.
Your virile bushes;
Much less inhabited.
Your smiling hopeful visage
Is the ink that pens this message…

66| Canada

Cold and clean
Oh Canada, Canada
Streets of marble
And terrain ever cold.
Your people busy
Subways chilly and clean
And eyes blue and wet.
In these speechless elevators,
Behold avenues,
Swept and candy sellers
Malls crammed and full
And men seem confused.
Canada,
Land of opportunities.
And Canada
Is cold and clean.

67| **Black Africa**

To you my darling mother,
My one and only
And I don't have another.
My dear family
Has entreated me not to
Ignore history
And our own origins, too.
This is our story
I tell in tears and sorrow
And it offends us
Deep into our bone marrow
After as soon as
They notice that we are black
And color doesn't cheat,
They also think our blood is dark.

We may take the heat,
But we have been strong
To speak to their face
That all along they are wrong
Since we know that race
Speaks volume of variety
And none is superior
Or all-wise in entirety
To think inferior
Of others who are diverse
When you reason in reverse
That today's culture
Is mixed civilization
Of a past nature;
Think Africa's ideation!

Sing you in skins dark
For there's no color as black!

68| Over the Seas

Here my people, I write
From over the seas, I write
To people dark and lovely,
May I write.

I am yours from abroad
I am a patriot and a child
Your own blood
A product of your need.

To my motherland,
In the fair and brown land
A place of civilization's splendor
And birth place of culture's grandeur.

Here they come to seek fortune
In the lands of fruits and pearls
Where music never lacks in tune
And women keep long hairs.

I am yours from overseas,
My name I have not changed,
Though I be gratified abroad
Yet my wish I will not alter.

My people, I write
And yours still I am
Even from over the seas.

69| Christian Nation

My country is a Christian nation,
A declaration of the century
A transition indeed
To the people in need.

My country is a Christian nation,
A declaration of good faith
A transition indeed
To a people who read.

My country is a Christian nation,
A declaration of trust
A transition indeed
To a people who hate greed.

My country is a Christian nation,
A declaration to God's glory
A transition indeed
To a people great in deed.

70| My Canada

Here my Canada I come.
Once visited forever treasured
Your nakedness is picturesque
Which haunt even in dreams.

Here in my Canada I am
Flesh stuck closer to flesh
Bones big, broad and hard,
Canada, may I call you mine?

Canada, the world's baby-sitter
Hope of the world's destitute
And Canada your open arms
Many a soul you protect.

Here my Canada I come
To breed light from darkness
And brood over unborn bloods
And Canada, I call you mine.

71| Heroes of Freedom

They fought as a band of soldiers;
They died while fighting, as martyrs,
Some are presidents if they lived,
And others have scars to show for.

We meet them daily in grey hairs
These are our truest statesmen,
These our prized gallant fighters,
Pillars on which we live and thrive.

We their brood their glory will save
Never to forget the blood they shed,
And in their footsteps we will follow,
Attesting to hearts strong and brave.

This freedom so for granted we take
With sword and pain was achieved,
Even when many in pieces returned,
Silently, yet very clearly they speak.

In libraries their heroism archived,
In pain and anguish they travailed,
These sons of liberty are of renown,
Heroes of peace, our true veterans!

72| Heathrow

Heathrow, Heathrow, Heathrow,
Though bright and ruddy
A detention thou art not
Let me pass, and let me go.

Thy skies in raining tears
Though thy summers be bright
A destination thou art not
Give me a pass, trip thy door.

Heathrow thou pride of London
Though mine luggage thou lost
A habitation thou art not
Bring me past thee, let me fly.

Heathrow, thy arms wide open
Though terrorists thou perturb
An occupation thou art not
Take my low past, push me high.

73| Over Paris

The skies of the ground beneath
The clouds within which we bracket
And though dull, pale and chalky,
The skies over Paris are bluest.

The envelop that canopies France
Opening its eyes towards Londres
And closing its mind to America
Is frisky, risky, milky and murky!

Oh, the feeling within the steel bird,
Oh, how magnificent it is inside,
Oh, how fearful and uncertain,
How trepid within these tempests!

Over the skies of great Paris
The sun shines lazily pale
In tints of orange and yellow
How relaxed is the air over Paris!

74| Mr. Thairu

Your tag read Richard Thairu,
At Jomo Kenyatta Airport
In the double lines of duty
When you paid no attention.

I am the one you mistreated
A vacationer you offended,
When you pushed me aside
Because like you, I am black.

Your tag said James Smith
At Dallas Fort Worth Airport
In the duty of two lines
When you paid much attention.

I have not forgotten at all
I was only a poor tourist
When you pulled me aside
Since unlike you, I am black.

People will many a time
Judge us by our simple looks
And only God all the time
Writes our truth in his books.

75| Kingdom Within

Man is a kingdom decked within.
The realm therein he aptly rules
With dignity and decorum
And dreams never in short supply.

Your own tender sleep, dreamy man
Will scout for reaching very far
And take you to lands far-away
Lands with plenty and yet unknown.

In your head above, thinking man,
These lands undiscovered are near
Full of treasure and raw riches
And so real and very well-known.

When you came across a signal
And vividly remembered that
You had existed there before now,
It was meetings of intuition.

And so many times you do dream
Of lands and peoples and places
Of plays and drama arenas
And of actors and actresses.

On these arenas and play stages
You have seen yourself escorted
By retinue clad in pure white
Whereas doors everywhere open.

You should never stop to believe
In the dreams of night and of day
For they portend hidden senses
And foretell future realities.

76| Perfect Full -Stop

Many days stop me and inquire
And there seem to be conference
Going on in the inside of me.
It is this keeping me searching
For the idyll time and right place
Where the 'I' in me would surface
And join me to self-made heroes.

Perfect full stop
When my sentence
Shall be completed,
What will its *predicate* be?
Will it have
A perfect summary of my life?

Many people need where to lean
Someone who looks out just for them
Who has themselves been there before
And by patience and endurance
Has come back home with life's trophies;
This someone must not be the end
But is only a stepping-stone.

Perfect full stop
When my sentence
Shall be completed,
What will its *object* be?
Will it have
A perfect summary of my life?

Many people at life's apex
Do say they began from somewhere
By trying out what was inside them.
Many of them discovered treasures
Of stuff they didn't think existed.
Someday we will find that someone
Who gives us wings with which to fly.

Perfect full stop
When my sentence
Shall be completed,
What will its *subject* be?
Will it have
A perfect summary of my life?

Many dark seasons do appear
To intimidate our courage.
Years of seed-planting will also come
To call for planning and hard work.
Times of helpful disappointment
And radical opposition
Break up eaglets from growing chicks
And make us who we really are.

Perfect full stop
When my sentence
Shall be completed,
What will its *statement* be?
Will it have
A perfect summary of my life?

77| Congo

Congo, thou land of biting gold
Thou crafted my father a home
And gave his son a wife am told
Congo, thou hast shrunken in form!

Thy womb bore many great children
Thy fortunes with them gladly shared
And though to thee they were foreign
Thine barrier was not closed or sheared.

The copper fields of Katanga
By which mine folks thou ably saved
From disgrace and piercing hunger
And their deficiency thou waved.

In thine rivers flow brooding blood
And thine skies drop toxic bullets.
Funeral songs are washed in flood
Horded with parts marred by mallets.

Congo, from my Zambia I call
From my terra firma I bawl
Congo, from Canada I declare
End thee thy ugly wars, I decree!

78| Idyll Phonoriah

These sounds
Smell of grapes
And of spices
Of great Indiana.
This is the place
Where we have to discover
Stories yet to be told.

We shall dance
To celebrate an idyll future
Of infectious flavors
And decorations in antique.
It is a country so bright
And land so light.

Oh, Phonoriah
A land so good,
A future so promising.
Oh, Phonoriah,
What an idyll a place!

79| Chitambo

Passing by Chitambo we saw a tomb
Whose epitaph was a dual petition
To the god of the feast of Hecatomb,
Written below was a re-petition.

He passed away with hands in akimbo
After braving the nip of fillaria,
And shunning many calls from the limbo
But was met by a shell of malaria.

This man bemoaned a German war Gotha
And found a panacea in helpful Chuma
Whom he taught the secrets of Golgotha
Whose blood-flow cures the tumor of Guma.

We hear sounds rattle from clouds in Congo
Sending dark and heavy rains of defiance
Smashing civilizations as ingle,
Washing them out without any reliance.

We come home back to village Chitambo
To water the plants of our great Sambo
Whom we rhyme in our book about poetics
Who savors the African politics.

Africa is now a Cinderella
Her beauty should not be spurned as loveless
And a reed-mat shouldn't be her umbrella
And she shouldn't be let to hold sap gloveless.

80| Mr. Conductor

You drive on tars of Beirut Road
Full of risks and wavy potholes
There you are on your way with loads
Filled with rage and stumbling on poles.

When that woman gullied on you
You almost lost a customer
But today you had just a few
So you just fixed your sad stoma.

At four every day you get up
And by twenty you are late on
For you rarely capture a nap
Nor find time to answer your phone.

In your busy life friends are few
Since they cannot see or know you
As you leave early and come late
Carrying out routines that you hate.

81| Tragic Song

The vile wars of Banguanaland:
Let me lament for the beloved
And compose a dirge to her plot.

My beloved has a spacious land
Sited between two great waters
Of Indian and Atlantic seas.

She dug it up and cleared out stones
And planted therein dire landmines;
She built a loom and secured it.

She dug around mass shallow graves.
Expecting to bring on power,
But alas, it brought gushing blood.

Dear kindred of civilized worlds
From Cape, to Freetown, to Khartoum,
From London to New York and past:

Did you observe the kid soldiers
Who are forced to drink human blood
And are strained to eat human fresh?

Wambo is factory to limbs;
My beloved's airs are polluted
With gases of ruinous rockets.

Who makes such planes in such plenty?
In whose interest are they shaped?
And who fashion rifles *en* mass?

Wars fought on my beloved's top soil
Have tainted its fertility
And rendered its earth impotent.

They die unceremoniously
And are buried without prayer
An offence to God, their Creator.

Refugee camps stripe my beloved
Just like the skin of a leopard
And the world believes it is free!

Poverty, like locusts, invades,
Ballots are nothing but a ruse
While laws only favor the rich!

The nations fob watch from a mile
And monitor as man kills man
And thinks it will never haunt them!

People in Banguanaland bawl:
Guiltless children worriedly howl,
But do you hear their hopeless roar?

82| War Sonnet

The gruesome visage of colorless war
And every time it stares its gape of woe
Into the fragile lives of the mortals,
It erodes a million hopes in totals
And render numerous desires devoid.
In gloom man reaps what he tend to avoid,
And in vain he gathers the world to moot
But always overlook war's evil root.
Is it not due to his queer lust and greed,
Of which he has forever vowed to breed
That the scarlet fluid of the innocent
Has flown into a sacrilegious waste?
The joy of life is damped hundred percent;
For gory wars instill in man the worst!

83| Rwanda

Rwanda, the core of Africa
Inserted between giant nations
What, shall I recount your sad fate?
The doom of oval-shaped people,
A society of ocean smiles!

Genocide, legacy of war:
A story I must tell with tears,
Rwanda, we will never forget,
We will never remain silent;
We won't deny you compassion!

You are now home to *infamy*,
Your survivors will not forget
The middle of the silent night
Which turned into an awry sight
Of the bloody massacre spree!

Rwanda, trees mature in straight lines,
Character of serenity
And outlook in tranquility,
But your citizens you murder
Hutus and Tutsis, you butcher!

Oh, horror, cry sacrilegious!
The unspeakable has happened,
Woe to the angel of dark Hades;
A strong nation you break apart
Just because their noses are different!

Rwanda, all innocently slain,
Your tragedy, is disaster,
A flaw in human decency,
A crime against humanity,
And error in human judgment!

84| Worst Antilife Report

Speak to me…
About war being won and lost;
About war separating everlasting friends,
And derailing further the amity of fiends!

Speak to me…
About ominous motives of terrorists;
About the perpetrators of homicides,
And about the perpetuators in genocides!

Speak to me…
About firing at unarmed and helpless people;
About what happens when the masses retire to sleep,
And the workers of anarchy awake to reap!

Speak to me…
About the flawless blood that flows;
About the unborn in volatile wombs,
And when they are born into jaws' tombs!

Speak to me...
About dignity when it is thwarted;
About the rights of the multitudes;
And of those who suffer the wrath of evil attitudes!

Speak to me...
About powers that disregard the song of peace;
About those who rush to pull the swords,
And do not attempt the soft power of words!

Speak to me...
About humans butchered like fowl;
About those in the name of patriotism
And who have done acts worse than nepotism!

85| Adventures

Sitting down on McDonald's pallor
At City Schipol International Airport,
In the old land of the Dutch legion:
I wonder that the day rolls away;
I wonder that I should have
Written many lines of rhyme;
I wonder that I have not started
An introduction to a book I would title
Simply as: *Adventures*.

People on scholarships travel far and wide
With cash in their bags;
But I travel with dreams in my head.
I travel on my own volition
In airplanes large and small.
In these unsponsored travels
I land on airports large and small.
In these adventures I look like a
Very Important Person or VIP,
Just like a president or prime minister;
But even though I am not all that,
The adventure, is still mine!

86| Schipol

Runways at Schipol are foggy
Byways, wet and straight and saggy
Weather, damp and dreary at most
Hazing birds and planes in the frost.

Rains fall in bits very softly
Temperatures are rising lofty
And steel shadows come and take off
To move the best in worlds of golf.

The queues, long and coiled like serpents
Flaunting badges of exotic merchants
And from neighborhoods of Deutschland
Cabs pass stunk strippers of Holland.

The simmering breathe grapples you
And shakes of hands are far and few
As friends and fiends rub hot shoulders
Fleeing Netherlands from closed borders.

87| **Bernados**

You need Canada,
And Canada also needs you:

Thus the anthem rung very early
At the dawn of civilization
At the expense of neglected childhood
When the call that saved Europe
And erected the ladder to prosperity
Was never equaled to elsewhere.

There along the corridors of Liverpool
Naked boys and girls
Squeezed in tiny squirms at Bernados
In need of food and shelter.

And Canada was open
To extend her hand
To the rescue of a genius posterity
And the legacy of goodwill
Which now and always
Great Canada is known by.

By the wood structures in Halifax
By night or by day via Quebec City
And worn-out from ancient labor,
Inhabitants of the world
Found the warmth in work
Denied them from Great Britain
And available to children
Who were neither exclusive workers
Nor bonafide members of their families.

88| Brutus

Clap your hands all you people
And shout for joy with a voice of triumph
For the mighty have fallen!
Oh, how they have fallen, the mighty!

Hussein is incarcerated
And Bush is deified
Just like Brutus murdered Caesar
With a sharp blade of a sword.

Saddam has murdered peace
With the face of the Iraq people

And George has butchered morality
With the vanity of the United Nations.

There at the Capitol
Great Julius Caesar fell
At the hands of him that he loved.

And at Capital Hill
The voice of the Security Council
Is silent, guilty of *vocaphobia*
A disease too hard to cure.

The rhythm of warfare
Has sent conflicting signals:

To aggressors, romanticism
While to the victim, it is realism.

You thought wrong
That the brute quest of Brutus
Did end with the defeat
Of the Triumvirate!

89| Canada, O Country

From east coast to coast to west coast
Three seas, gigantic waters boast
At the confluence of the seasons
Dress'd therein as queen of reasons
Bordered by ten decked retinue
Canada, a group's revenue!

From cold to mild cold to deep cold
Whiter than a glass of pure gold
The hollers of pulping maples
Fall along the trees for apples
To hide the pale-shaded meadows
From shrilly and wintry shadows!

From one nation to another
Here all freely came to gather
From Pacific to Atlantic
Buzz anthems novel and antique
Of "O, Canada, Our Country,"
In both English and French poetry!

90| First Black

Thou hast trodden the path long paved
By the blood of civil rights' throng
Of which Dr. King civil struggles saved
Though the road was dark and long

Thy long walk to white house's glory
Did not in the right's movement begin
Though Selma to Montgomery
An open door it ushered in.

A savior in chic Obama
Rare, wise and uncommonly born;
Fluent in speech and sane in karma
What fêted an event he won?

Over the top of Mount Pisgah
There the good Lord retired Moses
And raised Luther King to trigger
A crown on first of black bosses.

91| Democracy

The womb of democracy has twins:
One is freedom, another is peace
And a nation which enjoys both wins
While those nations devoid of it miss.

There is a session of spanking air,
When people can freely make a choice
From elections held freely and fair,
An exact expression of their voice.

A people in their natures fallen
An apt manager that they must choose
Their liberties portly and swollen
He must further, bribes he must refuse.

There are regimes power abuses
They do contain, and rights they foster.
A rule, fraud it never amuses
While its record prove, by a pollster.

By itself democracy isn't best
Only that all other forms of rule
Which were finer or better or first
Have been inferior and never true.

The strength of a good democracy
Is not in a first-rate theocracy
But in values of institutions
And the rule by its constitutions.

92| Tip of Africa

At the tip of Africa,
What hilarity and grandeur!
The temperate west coasts
Of the lovely eastern grooves,
The sea, the rivers and oceans,
All together weave
Into a lovely impression.

The land of light and beauty;
You have come to South Africa,
The people in carefree moods
In houses paneled and lofty
By black and blue labors.

You hear the sounds of cars
And see the noises they create:
The best places are here
Where life goes to the brim
In the heart of Johannesburg,
The world's city.

Here are buried in rands, gold
And its display
In splendorous Eaton center.
South of Africa
Is a-free-country,
A continent at the tip of Africa.

93| **Epidemics**

Oh Aids, menace killer, pale, ugly!
No longer a regular visitor
But an on-the-loose stooge.
You have aggravated immunities
And robbed live communities.

You are an ephemera,
Striking with ephemeral speed,
Among the favorites of men.
You and cancer,
Refuse to grant life its properties
And deny old-age its liberties.

Two displaced beasts
Afflicting joys and inflicting blows;
You have broken human cells
With lethal force
And there is no place, space, or race
Where you have not raked your face.

Assiduous fighting men
Fighters of deadly agendas;
Our patrons in medicine
Refuse to accept your subtle drill
And in time your sting will chill.

94| Inside a Genocide

Sing not on thy bed to thy child
Who thou did not attempt to chide
For the evil that brews within him
Finds a pathway and spills the rim.

They christen it ethnic cleansing
With raised guns and axes they sing
When their fellow man is hunted
While heroic war hymnals chanted

Who dares to scream bloody murder!
To bring the fierce monster under?
Thou discount sounds of genocide
And thy virtue thou cast aside

The guiltless souls of the maimed dead
And sights of remains beheaded
In mass but shallow graves stench
While justice reckons on her bench.

For Rwanda, let the rivers say
And Darfur, the sands will spay
Cambodian fields will not bargain
And halls of gas cry, "Never Again!"

BOOK FOUR

ODE TO AUSHI WOMEN

It is not vain-glory for a man [or woman]
and his glass to confer in his own chamber

- Shakespeare

95| Ode to Aushi Women

In the area of Luapula
The nut-growing marsh of Mansa
Drums loudly beat on scapula,
Whence flat bottoms are but cancer!

She is just a small tender girl
You can count her black pubic hair
Her chest empty like a funnel
While her nipples are red and bare.

She prods on Bangueulu plateaux
With silly gazelle-like blushes;
She only prefers troupes of twos
With virgin peers in the bushes.

The rare wisdom of her betters
Has not yet charmed her frail figure;
She is shy through her dried fetters
And her lips are out and bigger.

She is not a woman, per say
Her blood is still cold and impure
Because the moon is far away
To chaste her fresh and to endure.

She has not danced *Infunkutu,*
The arrangement of three drums,
The ancient rhythm from Timbuktu;
Nor won the dry skins of wild rams.

She will be taught *Akalela*
To learn how to open taut legs
And she will know *Amalela*
To make kids from fertilized eggs.

They will soak her in *Munwa* stream
To broaden her pelvis
And fulfill her childhood dream;
To break the curse of a novice.

The sweet juice of soundless rivers
Elongates her womanly shaft
To cure every natural fevers
And purge the lucky winner's haft.

Her sully frame will be made firm
Decked with *Kolwe's* pure diadems
To date, she has well-run her term
And will earn the prize of rare gems.

Outside, she is cramped with shivers;
Her life's canal is perfected
And her full pulse proudly quivers;
But her self is unaffected.

Her body is bottle in form,
Her nipples are now hard and full,
Her buttocks are firm and uniform
And her waist is mellow to pull!

She has been accepted by Ra
Goddess of the erect solar,
And the shining fruit goes to her,
To court gods of the other polar.

She's joined the Aushi women's core
Who cause charcoal to burn brightly
And make impotent nobles whole,
To mix blood and water rightly.

She can now handle Mandingo,
The killer of angry male lions,
That dancer of the hailed tango
Who with just bare hands breaks irons!

Prefer we the Aushi women
With their ever protruding backs
Which confuse sanity in men
And accord night the force it lacks.

Their place in humanity
Loses its share in virility,
Gains it in masculinity
And modes it in fertility!

She kills the eyes of on-lookers
And she is not for press showings.
Suitors treasure her like vodkas
And her heart beats higher than wings.

Do not expose her publicly;
Her nude was made for great virtues.
They pass-out rather too quickly;
Those who resist, become statues.

A love son of Luapula soil
Has never known to marry two.
Legend has it that he will toil
And his garden, he will not do.

Oh these Luapula Aushi curves,
How succulent their deep bosom,
In which mankind vibrates life's waves
And men's desires bloom and blossom!

Sing to her gyrating shifts
And swing through her softly paired rifts.
Mark nimbly her alluring nod
And mate safely in fleshly gold.

BOOK FIVE

SONGS OF AN ALIEN

When one realizes that his life is worthless
he either commits suicide or travels

- Edward Dahlberg

Song 1| Sweet Name

Sweet is your name to my memory
Smooth to my clean shaven cheeks.
Did I tell you I knew about you
When in sense and word we rhymed?
You were my morning brightening star
A song I sang when I knew not how.
I saw your face always in phases,
When you smiled without blinking,
And spoke without moving upper lips.

Sound are my dreams when I fall asleep
Saying your name repeatedly and softly.
You were right when you kissed me
And not wrong when I held you back.
But it is your heart that I adore;
Your smiles that dropped spotless love –
For while many friends I have had,
To find one like you is truly hard!

Song 2| Broken Lullaby

Stranger your tongue and tone is a broken lullaby
For before we had time to talk, we said goodbye.

I have met many who look like you, and have said
"hi!"
Only to discover they are not you when they sigh.

I have tried to forget about you and reach very high
But when your frame illuminates mine, I say, "my,
my!"

We were like sister and a brother when we shared a
pie
But you knew to me you were not just but another
guy.

One thing you didn't want me to do, I don't know
why
You never let me stroke your knuckles or let me try.

You were an angel who brightened my very blue sky
And carved the wings with which I was able to fly.

Song 3| Subway

Thank you subway in which my mind comes to life.
For in you I hatch poetry beautiful and sensual.
You fill my heart's chamber with precious thoughts
And chip my hands with fruitful narratives.
At St. George myriads disembark in high heels
As bells and sirens cloud my ripen memory!
I hear the chuckles of young nightingales
And pay attention to the songs they sing.
Kennedy to Kipling sings my soul in pure verse
As I recite the sweet numbers of divine crescendo.
In staccatos of blank and rhymed lines
I find my being and the reason I live.
Oh, you gods that rule in these darkly tunnels,
Muses who sharpen my linguistic genius –
Stand at Bay when Castle and Frank broadly view
And all veterans keep and protect at War-den.
Strange is when life abundantly flows at Keele,
While guns and brains are traded for favour at Jane!

Song 4| Love-Marriage Mystery

Stranger to the world of love and deep feelings
Struggling to understand why we do things.
I saw a girl that I thought would marry me;
I slapped the flakes when it was not to be.
Is it only fantasies that our ideals faint?
Are there proofs that its dreams that we paint?
Reading through lives of human stories,
Realizing that they are just forsaken glories -
For every good two people that will marry,
Foremost will be to kill their ex's and burry.
Yet their memories will never escape at all,
Yelling aloud in their absent-minded chore.
It is the sound of heavy drops of tears,
Eating nerves and awakening myriads of fears.
Why do we change shirts like soccer players?
Willing to live with products of unmet prayers?
Oh, the mystery of marriage and love,
Only God truly knows what's true and above?

Song 5| Goma Lakes

Besides the still waters of the Goma Lakes,
There we strutted silently in search of fortunes.
Movements in sacredly displayed bumble sashes,
In green lands of well groomed marshlands.
Here in silent thoughts, we hatched future lives;
Our minds ran deeply, and our studies gained thrust.
There at the great university uncertainties loomed
As our graduation days grew thinner and closer;
Men and boys here came together of age
While girls and women kicked in tight jeans.

Goma Lakes, our heart and soul:
With every ripple a circle of avowed expectations
And every drop, a thought of anticipated vocations.
By the serene water fronts, our fears turned to joy
While our vanities told us we were still learners.
The level of every rescinding depth
Summed up our desire to overcome retention,
And fallen branches made our temporary bridges.
Oh, Goma Lakes, where our betters crossed
Before their day of jubilation, they celebrated!

Goma Lakes - your tall straight trees
Shall account for all the plans
Which besides your oasis, have been made.
Your caves of rounded bush and pricking barbs,
Hide deep secrets of broken virginities.
We shall come back to Goma Lakes
To vindicate our pasts now forgotten
And rejoice over pleasures that eluded us
Here at Goma Lakes, we find healing charms;
Besides the Goma Lakes, our hopes live again.
Here, our stories developed plot lines
And secured us from republics of cruel fines!

Song 6| Sun

Sun when you are tiring, do so fast;
When you awake, blow no trumpets.
My people live under brimming rays;
Under the guise of licking roofs!
The meek darked-hearts share space
To rise from rage and pain of struggle,
Seeking for safety in a wrong place!

Sun on my people you shine last;
After exhausting all your strength!
You bring feeble rays of nutrients
To calm minds weak and hands limp.
Children fumble in filthy streets
Begging for food in stinking basins.

Sun, set and don't blame it on the past;
Neglecting hope on the sea of trouble.
Your light turns to mourning
And stories become weapons of failure.
They fall so deep in the pit of misery
And no-one braves to rescue them.

Sun close not your eyes on the just;
Darkness hides its devious deeds
In royal lies and eloquent speeches
While rulers build futures and chalets
Where they hoard pearls and treasure
To feed their gigantic appetites
With empty hearts and packed heads!

Song 7| **Mantras**

Alien you brag, even spite yourself
That slavery had its part in antiquity.
You rave at the mention of its breaking
Claiming the ancient minds boo-booed.

You are not alone, many are just like you
Who serve frustrated bosses
And pal around with industrial superiors
Who thwart laws of ergonomics.

Rules in the executive boardroom
Ring a different tune from those on the floor.
Pain and its cousin, broken joys
Wrangle incessantly in disgruntled lines.

At shipping and receiving stations
Paper and palm-tracks crambo through coils
Irritating already fragile eardrums
Caused by years of repeated motions.

Breathless hearts pound into warehouses,
Ignoring blood is thinner than diesel,
While shaven bosses lax through idly,
Imbibing coffee and chanting mantras.

Song 8| Wealth

Oh wealth, oh money, oh riches!
Oh mighty, oh power, oh strength!
Oh wealth – do not deny me
Oh money – do not elude me
Oh, if you can, embrace me
Oh, I beg, do not forsake me.

I know the merciless heart of lack
And the miserable hand of poverty
In both, human dignity retreats
And stiff hands of embarrassment rule
Sense and reason take an easy way
And knowledge is a beggar's whip.

I have asked you, lover of none
And beseeched your counsel,
Accepter of all
Because in you,
Wit and foolhardy trust
And fame answers only to you.

Song 9| Chaisa

Chaisa, oh Chaisa, how poor a place
The thought of you breaks my heart
Oh Chaisa, how dusty your streets.

Chaisa, women carry two pairs of shoes
And wish churches have two washrooms
Little army cling to ivory-legged limbs
And would not give up to strong winds.

Chaisa, men travel with polish brushes
And boys wear camouflaged dustcoats.
Chaisa, your houses have no foundations
Catching easy colds from heavy tropics.

How can I forget you, in your lowly hour?
Or forsake you, when you need power?
Chaisa, how can I your desolation ignore
When in dirt and dust you lay low?

Song 10| Northern Hemisphere

I sing to your beautiful skies and days
Oh universe of the magnificent North!
As a child I only thought of rains
And sun-scotched patches of October.
In visions, wisdom slept pale;
In endless whispers of love.
The posts of the universe in twos posit,
Walking between thickets of dry sands
And reaching white and chilly valleys.
Our minds race infantile fantasies -
Comparing you only to Aphrodite.
A child in terror-ripped village
Vowed to drown the darling of South
Calling her Snow and Mirage.

Song 11| Feeble Rights

It is obvious and I can see it in your mind
As you walk, aimlessly and eyes down.
You are always thinking as you walk
And this you do day and night.
You never straighten up your head
And your steps are always disoriented.
Even in the flurry of spring,
Your eyes are still small and squeezed.
You walk as if you are hiding something
And your own salutes betray you.
You are an alien, better you admit it
Or those who lent you feeble rights
Confiscate the little you have.
The streets on which you trot
Are hard and cold, very cold.
They were manufactured from bitumen
Acquired from the sweat of slave labor
The labor of vindictiveness.
The peace of the world you do not have
And neither do you possess joy.
You claim you stay in a paneled house,
Which is but a refreshing station
And a changing room
To which you only return at mid-night
To munch hard crusts of bread
Since you have no time to cook,
And early in the morning,
You run the monstrous machines
Which neither retire nor rest.

Song 12| Weird Thinking

The plight of an alien is his platitude.
You left your own country with a quest
Hoping to find gold scattered in the
Polished boulevards of trekkersland.
You had thought your own peoples
Were ruined and uncivilized,
You have used the term "backwards"
Time and again, as if your people
Aren't even trying to make progress.
Prisoner of your own weird thinking,
Is almost suitable to you,
And your own languid motives cheat you.
You are never content, never satisfied.
Some people have better manners,
And better manners are bedrocks of
Candid civilizations.
Some people display mature ways of life
And do not ignorantly offend others
In the lands in which they are aliens.
Some are aliens on grants,
The benefits of which will never
Develop their deserted nations.
There were opportunities you never saw
In the land in which you claim
Nothing developmental goes on.
But now you say,
How I will be rich
When I return to my own country;
Such hypocrisy is huge,
Since kings are born, and not made.

Song 13| Industrial Towns

I see the rains pouring steadily outside.
The land is being watered for cultivation
And you are wondering why the waste
Since no clear land exists,
Only silhouetted towers and skyscrapers.
No pigsties exist, too,
Only idyll havens
Full of electronically operated motors.
There is no hoe for agriculture, either.
They have combine harvesters,
And long honked tracks and tractors
Which bring in corn, wheat and rice
In bulk supplies for sale and export.
There are transit carriers and long buses
Carrying busy and disheveled men
And blond and brunette women.
Industrial power is auto-run
While human labor works them in shifts
And their din never fades.
Such is the state of affairs in these
Industrial towns where gold is unheard of.
Alien, you only see automobiles
Which are feminine
Since their owners treasure them more
Than they care for their wives.
Cars outnumber the traveling public
And the outnumbered, control traffic rights.
Alien, you see all the beautiful surroundings
And they don't belong to anyone
As owners have not paid for mortgages.

Song 14| Free Existence

An alien, is he only so because of birth?
If we should allow him to obey laws
Just as citizens do,
Can't we also allow him to exist freely?
An alien is a dreamer,
Always dreaming of threats of relocation.
What if he does not have anywhere to go?
If his native land is infested by plagues
Or is invaded by other foreigners,
Or worse still, canopied by battle planes?
Is it only lack or poverty,
That pushes an alien to voyage?
He sees innocent policemen in dreams
Coming towards him and asking for papers,
Demanding that he shows them evidence
That he came in through right means.

By right means, they do not mean
Coming by chartered flights
Or in luxurious greyhounds,
But with authorization by the
Consulate of the nations
Which, too, exist in the alien's country.
They talk about law and order and cops.
They count the alien's steps and
Ensure that he does not exceed the limit.
Yet you seem to understand law and order
And you are more law-abiding than
The citizens of the nation in which
You seek refugee.
If you are law-abiding,
Why do you still think you are a foreigner?

Song 15| Dreams of an Alien

The dreams of an alien are weapons,
Horrendous and lethal.
His night visions are invisible
And well-plotted.
In his dreams, an alien can be free,
Free from fear of relocation and trespass.
In his night visions he can buy a house,
Find great a job and be an executive.
In his dreams all plants are green,
And all roads lead to bliss.
In these exotics all scenes are in summer,
No winter inconveniences,
And all settings are in late spring
With beautiful surroundings and flowers;
And all flowers are either daisies or roses,
And all roses are red and white.
But he wakes up, all about him
Is either blurred or suffocated;
How he longs for the night
When he can fall again and fantasize
And reach places
Too difficult for commoners,
And wear clothes
Too expensive for the jobless.
An alien's dreams are sweet, too.
In the best of deep dreaming,
Ideas are laid and hatched in full,
Bearing green leaves and yellow fruits.
Here he is not imprisoned by his reason
But liberated by it.

Song 16| Schizophrenic

An alien is accused of being schizophrenic,
A mental disorder of ambivalence.
He is made to behave like one
Because he does not have enough sleep.
A man with rights is a small god,
Able to recreate and reproduce.
But a foreigner is like an impotent rich ruler.

"Once there lived an impotent emperor,
Who, due to sheer vanity,
Added one concubine to the numbers yearly.
The thing in between was but a haunch.
The young charmed maidens were wasting
Inside the marble palace.
They peeped through narrow lintels
For the courtiers who wear no silky apparel
And feed on no dignified a table.
Yet they have living hernias.
He was a king with a populous kingdom,
Extending from coast to coast,
And his queens lay flat-bellied
As flat as the king's own dining table!"

So is an alien, in the land in which
His abilities are despised and ignored.

Song 17| Hope

An alien counsels, do not underestimate
The power of hope because hope outlives.
Hope in the land where you never wasted
Your umbilical cord.
Hope is a living thing; and has a heart.
Hope passes current inconveniences
And brings valued agendas to the brim.

"I hope in these hopeless terrains
Of landlessness.
In the midst of failure, l have seen success,
And I can reason why.
I walk with eyes down, an open mind and
With eclectic thoughts.
I allow not my independence to betray me."

Though the land where you live is not yours,
Do not despise your economic potential.
It cannot be hijacked, but gives you power,
The ability to procreate and improve others.
Do not be reduced to a pathetic loafer,
And that, not even in your matrimonial bed.
But write books, on poetry or romance
And sell them on the internet or bookstores
And earn yourself a reasonable living.
In that way, you can sit down
And let your talents feed you.

Song 18| Rich People

The alien advises, there are rich people
And people with riches.
Rich people are rare and few in number
Since they have to have rich minds.
People with riches are large in numbers
But riches find wings and fly away.
People go to work daily, yet only little benefit.
I learned this because
I was once looking for reality's old meaning
And stumbled on several laws of economics.
Streets are filled with movements of workers
Children go to fast restaurants for fatty foods.
They grow up obese or near to it
And are ashamed of themselves.
Others in nations where food is scarce
Deem it a blessing to be fat, even very fat.
When they get skinny,
They are ashamed of themselves
Because society might think
They suffer from incurable diseases.

Tax return brings future rebates.
I regret selling my house in my native land,
And now I move like a shadow
And a destitute in a foreign land.

"Time is Money" is true to the West
And "by grace we survive," is to the South.

Song 19| Critical Thinker

An alien is not a stranger to critical
Thinking; he does engage his mind
In productive reasoning.
Truth is what always wins and stays
Untainted and unadulterated.

"Once there was a man determined
To defeat truth. He introduced his
Arguments with lies and supported
Them with lies. Then one day his
First born son was born and medical
Officials told him that he was a girl.
He disputed the fact with truth
Because he saw that the baby
Had no female features on it
And he would not give his child
A girl's name. From that time on,
He respected truth and vowed
To say the truth and nothing
But the truth: and so God helped him!"

Charles Mwewa

A truthful plan is not devoid of ideas,
It can only be neglected.
It is truth that foreigners are,
By relativity, very wealthy.
There is truth that they live
To invest since they might be asked to
Leave for their countries.
In your own country, critical thinking
Is rare because all you see is familiar
To you and to everybody else.
You are shaped in a predictable form
And good ideas are not easily conceived.
Good plans are rubies in strange lands.

Song 20| Race of Women

I was a stranger to the race of women
Until I had tied a matrimonial knot.
Beautiful, elegant women are very strange,
And do they really exist in strange lands?
"Beauty is in the eyes of the beholder"
As it applies to women, is very deceptive.
For after one marries and stays with her,
He ceases to see her face,
However pretty it is,
Instead one begins to see her heart,
However hidden it might be.
Women are sophisticated from afar,
Nearer they are not.
Their charm is not on what they put on,
But in what they neglect.
From afar, her lips are red and dripping;
Her eyes are doves and flying;
Her mouth is watery and inviting;
Her curves are divine and enticing;
And her voice is soft, as calm as streams
Of the quiet waters.

But what you don't know about her
Is that she is a mystery,
As unpredictable as a chameleon.
Yet when she comes nearer,
And after you place her in your arms,
She is simply as delicate as rules of begging.
Those eyes are just large globes,
Empty sockets, but lively and beautiful
And strong men have paid for them.
She wears fashions of deceiving splendor
And you learn to love her
For the reality that you don't even know.

Song 21| Idle Mind

Oh, that I should be given something,
Cried an alien.
That I might not stay idle,
Loafing and eating the bread of laxity.
Work is the aim of life,
The bell that awakens conscience.
A worker owns the world in which
He toils and derives satisfaction from it.
In the pockets of work are
Three compartments;
One says *eat*, the other says *shelter*
And the last one says *clothe*.
These compartments are occupied
And when they are empty,
Untold miseries and pain come.
That is why a worker has
Found the bait to attract the three.
A loafer has not.

"One day a crazy man washed his
School books in the sink in order to
Soften his understanding of the subject.
He forgot that there is no nexus
Between paper and grey matter,
Though some papers may be grey.
In another institution of learning
A crazy student was found studying
With lights switched off. After the
Lights were switched on, he was seen
Busy in his books flapping pages
And making notes. Asked why he was
Studying in the dark, he replied that
He had no time to waste, day or night."

Song 22| Time

To be stranger to time is worse than
The sin of immorality.
Immorality, though,
Is a worst state of the heart.
Time helps us to demarcate a day
And helps our days flow smoothly,
And is essential to life.
Yet time brings anxiety and heartaches.
The realization that there is time
Is what forces the lazy to get up
But hard workers are deluded
By the idea that time eludes them!
The guilt that follows moments
Of time wasting are greater than
The pleasures that are achieved
As a result of doing little in much time.
There is time for everything and
No time for nothing.

That is why God has allowed people
To work in their dreams
Even though their bodies are dead.
In a place where everybody works
And time is as vital as the heart's state,
Find strength to spend eight
Or twelve hours of real work.
An alien from the land of the carefree
Will starve to death in a province
Where you earn a dollar hourly,
And not a salary for no work done at all.
Time spent at school is thus appreciated
As long as a salary
Honors your past school efforts.

Song 23| Good and Evil

A stranger warns; do not put your trust in mortal men
Born from the grotesque wombs of women.
Scientists too are not to be overtly trusted.
One of them once said,
"Evil and good are simply hypothetical ideas
And neither bad nor good people exist."
He perceives evil as a mental perspective
And yet our elders, who have seen much,
Dispute the fact as inconsistency.
Evil and good are the sciences of morality,
Which are to be learned empirically
And which also distinguish
Mature men and immature women from
Immature men and mature women.
To deny evil exists is to be evil personified
And to discard thrives to be good,
Is being truly unscientific.
Oh alien, poor alien,
Be a believer in truth and a disbeliever of evil
And in that you will prove the ancient slogan
That Darwin left hanging by simple postulations.
The 'unimpeachable' Evolution Theory is an enigma
To non-scientists and a mental grave to the religious
And both are not to be supposed.
To be professor with no good or bad notion
Is like being ridiculed for walking on the moon,
And this too is as a bath in concentrated acid.

Song 24| Rules of the Game

The alien is sworn to play by
"The Rules of the Game" and I say
Do not despise such cheap propaganda.
These are the essential mores
And dynamic social rules
Which have shaped our world
From time immemorial.
They have maintained a certain amount
Of social order and tranquility
And have squeezed delinquency
From sophisticated social misfits.

Advocates of our legal system
And enforcers of our laws
Are they trained to pursue or
Denigrate our earthly rights?
Do they defend or defeat law?
Do infidels escape while
The innocent are punished,
If it is not so, then tell me?
Cooked defenses are tasty,
More than prosecution procedures.
Acquittals on technicalities
And convictions on insufficiency of
Evidence are all ploys to deny justice
To men and women who cannot talk.
Yet we repair mitigations and allow
Evil to flourish in a world
In which felon is lawlessness
While defending of hard cores
Is quintessential professionalism.
Alien, seek to do justice, always!

Song 25| Rundlehorn Drive

The fantastic breeze just on
The onset of summer
In the inner corridor of Rundlehorn Drive
Behind Pinehill Street, Calgary, Alberta
Swells with sounds of remembrance.
The wetlands of Twatotela Crescent,
Overshadowed by light industrial dins,
In the land where God has never retired
And miners never go on annual vacations.
The feeling of summer is
Light to the blind soul
Awakening all the senses of ecstasy
And bringing joy to its full.
Oh, how I love these senses,
The sweet smells of after rains
Which have poured all night long
And soothe our feeling of trepidations.
This breeze is calm
And resonates with unexplained
Greatness and mildness
And Alberta's weather is unpredictable,
A strange reminder of the serenity
Of Zambia in the cold season.

Song 26| Fall from Purity

Why is it that your backyard is plane,
Like a can of beer, they are empty?
You stuff and fill it
With pieces of pink paper
So that when you walk
No lines follow your contours.
You have been complaining,
That one day you are going to
Dig out the entire road network
Because you have seen enough
Bodies and empty buttocks.
You complain that
Young girls are making you crazy.
That they have no manners because of
The way they dress which
Leave a lot to be desired.
Stop moving, alien,
Because what you have just seen
Is only a drop in an ocean.
You are yet to see
The winter of shameless nudes;
The spring of artificial breasts,
The summer of bizarre heights
And then you will fall from purity!

Song 27| Super Problems

Alien in the nation to which
You have proudly gone to settle,
Do not overlook the value of
Small nations around.
Do not say the land in which
I have graciously sought refuge
Is a super class super power.
For the rulers of the smaller
But peaceful nations
Will hear you and lecture you.
For there must be good leaders
To breed excellent followers.
But with the theory of
International politics
Big nations do not lead
Smaller nations because of
The doctrine of Sovereignty.
Yet the Republic of South Africa
Rules over the kingdoms of
Lesotho and Swaziland
With economic overloads.

The United States of America
Rules over Iraq and Afghanistan
With military overtones.
Alien, superpowers have
Super problems and small nations
May have huge economic potentials.
And do not be fooled:
Big nations will someday collapse
Just like Rome and Egypt did
And smaller nations will rise
Just when you least expect it!

Song 28| Emmerance

This is the word of wisdom
The alien gave to Emmerance
In the land in which
She was born,
A land which became hers
By virtue of birth,
And the land in which her
Umbilical cord was accurately
Cut and destroyed:

"To be truly free, my daughter,
Acquire knowledge and by it
Gain understanding, discretion,
Goodwill and prudence.

Do not wait for the money lovers
To offer you patterned knowledge,
The world around you shall be
Your classroom and nature
Shall tell you all you need to know.

Read books written by
Passionate researchers and
Do not despise the counsel
Of those who came before you.
Whenever your head gets stuck,
Do not be headstrong,
But rather lift up your eyes
To the skies where He lives.

True freedom, my well beloved,
Lies in knowing who you are
And respecting the rights of others."

Song 29| Clientele

I, an alien and a visitor in the land of
The mortals again and again ask this:
Do politicians play by the rules or against?
They amass lucrative wealth
At the expense of governable masses
And pretend to play patriotism
Only, and only when it befits them
And as quickly as they lose elections
They organize versatile protests.

Protocol. Politics. Power.

Apart from their plosive sounds,
What do they share in common, tell me?
They act on the stage of frail promises,
And are cheered for victories
They never initiated.
These are day-time robbers.

What more, should I talk about
Their "honorable titles,"
And the monopoly they demand
On sweat-earned national capital
Which they have grabbed
And registered in their names, far away!
This is strange,
And a chasing after wind.
Liars are attractive and unavoidable.
Extortionists are simple and organized,
No wonder they easily win the hearts
Of hard working citizens.
Has our world paid lip service
To the troubles of voiceless masses?

Song 30| Preachers and Politicians

They preach…
They teach
And loudly proclaim.
The pulpit and senate podiums
And parliament and church buildings are one.
The constitution,
And the Bible
Are both enforceable…
And exegesis and legal interpretation
Are similar
And so is the clientele for one,
The clergy,
The same as for the other,
The politician.
Promises…and the Word of God,
Reverberate in the ears of
The "faithfuls" in the name of God.
And the "faith-fools" are sulked
In the name of partisanship.
Actions are taken and judgments passed.

"Believe in the Lord and you will be saved,"
Declares one,
And, "Believe in the loan and receive low rates,"
Demands the other.
Give.
Give.
And "it shall be given back to you,"
Emphasizes the clergyman…
Give up,
Give up!
Give up what: property, rights?
Stresses the politician.

Song 31| Love Theorem

"Falling in love is chemical reaction,"
Retorts the chauvinist.
One can stay in love,
And the other can walk into it,
And marriage is a recipe for disaster
And the bigot does not know.
Love dies. And love lives.
Love is a predictable feeling.
And love has a life span.
And nobody seems to dispute all that,
A twenty first century love theorem
And a blatant one for that matter.
For the older generation,
Marriage is better than flirtation.
But for the novel generation,
Vacillation from partner to partner
Is not a specialization in promiscuity.
Fall in love.

And multiply the falling again and again
And then marry her, for God's sake,
And tell the coward to be brave
And tell him that he should marry!
To live with a woman,
Is definitely very hard indeed,
But to live without her
Is unarguably not what a man needs.
And this is the song, sing it again:
To the stranger, sing organized rhythms
And play the drums to deafness
And loudly declare, that divorce,
Is a tuneless symphony played by a
Disorganized orchestra.

Song 32| Money and Politics

Alien, in the foreign land where you go,
Several things you must remember
And one thing you should not forget:
That politics and life are twins;
They have existed alongside each other
For time and time immemorial.
Life is not run by politicians
But politics rule at the center of life
Money and politics
Are two sides of the same coin
Yet politics has hijacked its place
And relegated it to obscurity.
Be no stranger to cash
And embrace the chance to politick
Because money is the weapon of politics
And those that have it
Are tigers in their own jungles.
Business and charities
And non-governmental organizations
And the church and interest groups
Have joined forces, everywhere.
There's no place where their voice
Has not been heard and neither is money's.
Are politicians white washed tombs?
People appoint them; politics promote them.
And I am sure money will demote them.
Alien,
Join politics, like me,
But don't be a politician, like them.

Song 33| Boiling Soul

Why my soul you boil within me?
Why you constantly unsettle yourself?
Should I tread the canyons and deserts
To bring you the peace you deserve?

Peace swings like babies on pendulum
My soul groans like a pigeon
My blood boils furiously like a broiler
While I feel the measure of real drapes.

Is there solace for the troubled soul?
Is there moments when they can rest?
Is there a place quiet and peaceful?
Is there a place for souls in distress?

Yet I am weary and tired of just living
While my peers swim in chocolate dyes
And wear suits of green embroidery.
Is there peace for a man of many plans?

Song 34| Payday

Alien to the feelings that you desire,
To the dreams that pass by in the night.
There you sit in the center of burning fire
To absolve every punch without a fight,
And day lingers like a pitiful tear.
As memory holds her bowels tight
To run from shadows she must not fear.
Do you think night is dark, day bright?
They work better whose respect is for peer
Who frighten fear with a sense of might
And believe payday is very near
To inoculate lack and numb the bite!

Song 35| Woman's Side

A stranger I am to colds, and lengths,
And heights and widths,
To free sight, to climbs, and
To pocking noses.
Mine is not the stature of giants
Nor of the pride of
Easier-spelled names.
And yet in this proudly I stand;
In the bosom of a woman's side,
In the chamber of pulping nerves
And the path of flowing life!

On the wrong tunes, they have played
The dancers have not moved a step
Flat tires are sustained
By enlarging fondling
And soft voices of dying breathe.
There is no known sweetness as these,
No sense as six times these
Hidden fountains!
Their taste no man has ever despised
And in these embraces, dies the might
And surrenders vetted heroes!

Song 36| Bed Chamber

Alien to the ways of the bed chamber
Looking as one battered by seven harmers
Pulsing perfidiously in off and on modes
Being unable in manner or posture to recant.

Alien you neglected the waves of life
Like an impotent king with myriad virgins.
There is purpose in breathing deeply
And intimately in the process of nature.

Men use toys to bridge off the child guy
And women look for glories in gossip.
It is what they never say that hurts;
For women as men, fear to fail in bed.

These lives divine no viagras need
Virility rescinding nimbleness to feed
Their agile surging power in force to recede
Reducing procreativity in source and speed.

Song 37| Rulers

When rulers rule, they say great things.
Their voice is heard in motion and pictures;
Their name is called by imperials and kings.
In games by lot pairs crash in fixtures.

The known will soon end in quarterfinals;
The unknown will ascend to the grand trials.
Twelve men will compete for a prize tonight
And a numberless throng will give a cheer.

In their wallets and purses days rejoice
And their work place is a litter of grief.
Here is a man with justice he rules
Guiding minds and ideas to laughing tables.

Swerving chairs and plates in joy will cheer
To mark a season of mended hopes;
This for long has eluded their wishes
But with a vote of confidence will return.

Song 38| Ignorance

I was, ignorant of the race of all
Until I came to Toronto Airport lounge
Then I saw the world in a lamp of glitter.

I was, cheated by the illusions of race
Until I sat on transit's rocket wheels
Then I learned that people exist in colors.

I was, holding on to untruthful legends
Until I entered the mammoth subways
Then I realized variety has a name.

I was, afraid to talk my thoughts aloud
Until at Humber I entered a geniuses' class
Then I saw that brains respect no threats.

I was, disturbed by my foreign accent
Until I spoke words attractive and smooth
Then I knew that I was complete and human.

For the lessons we learn while awake
Strange they may be, yet short and true.

Song 39| Roundness of the Globe

"Do not gaze at me",
Began the alien,
"With those blue and brown eyes of yours.
I also have my own people, with a culture.
We were ten when we were born,
With seven strong boys and three girls.
We leaped through the jungle of life
With fried opinions and hammered lips
And found the world a stratum of classes.
Now I have lost all who were mine,
And that not through bullets or jaw-bones,
But through the roundness of the globe.
Yet I have this to my credit,
I love the smell of ink, and the
Bluntness of a pen, and my hands,
Are strings on a well-tuned violin."

Thus began and ended the
Curriculum vitae of the alien,
Whose brief account of his own
Qualification and previous occupation,
Does not exceed the thoughts
Of those around him,
And the job that he seeks
Is not in places their qualified delve.

Song 40| Epiloguia

The song of an alien, for the alien,
Has been sung in a foreign land
Where he has not belonged,
And to the people unfamiliar
And unappealing,
From the world of issues.

To munch a large elephant
Is the duty of everybody,
Because by its size, an elephant is huge.
One man picks one piece
And faithfully feeds it to another man
Who was left idling at home,
Yet the glory of the killer is unknown.

To kill a huge beast,
Allow it to swallow you alive first
Lest in-between its teeth you lie grounded.
In the land in which you are,
You are an alien, a visitor, a stranger.

Eat only the portion of your grass
And sleep only on the bed you have made
And plant seeds of benevolence
In order to reap fruits of good will
From honest plants of undaunted justice.
On this earth, we are all aliens
And many will be
The forces of alienation.
Through ink and *pain,*
We pen down our experiences
And sow seeds of love in others.